MW00880712

Happiness in Health Care

The power of positive attitude in patient care.

KRISTIN HALL

authorHOUSE®

AuthorHouse™
1663 Liberty Drive
Bloomington, IN 47403
www.authorhouse.com
Phone: 1-800-839-8640

First published by AuthorHouse 5/14/2010

ISBN: 978-1-4520-1849-2 (sc)

*Printed in the United States of America
Bloomington, Indiana*

This book is printed on acid-free paper.

How it all began

It was a typical Monday morning at a small hospital in southern Wisconsin, but what happened next was anything but ordinary and it would forever change my attitude and way of thinking. It was an honest question from the most negative, miserable person that I have ever met. I can still hear the brash tone of his voice as he boldly asked, "Why the hell are you so damn happy?"

Now, I am a very up-beat positive person with a sharp wit and usually quick to respond, but I had to think about this one for a second. "Why was I so happy? What makes me act so upbeat; is it simply my personality or something deeper?"

I think back to the first time I saw this patient. It was 6:30 A.M, shift change, and the time when the night shift informs the oncoming shift about their group of patients. Before meeting Leo for the first time I was told, "This guy will be your worst nightmare today. All he does is complain, yell, and swear at you. There is just no way to please this man. Good luck".

From that moment on, I was on a mission. I was going to find a way to make this guy smile or die trying. So, that day I spent extra time with Leo and asked him numerous questions, most of the time without getting a response other than "Mind your own damn business or shut the hell up". Leo's prognosis was not good. He had end stage renal failure and seemed to be getting worse by the day. Leo seemed to have very few people in his life that cared for him and even fewer that came to visit.

Days, weeks and months went by and each day that I worked, I would spend extra time with Leo. Sometimes I would simply tell him about my day and other times we would share stories from our past. Leo began to open up to me, and I, to him. Before long, my coworkers would inform me of the fact that Leo began asking where I was on the days that I didn't work. In a strange kind of way, it made me feel appreciated. That possibly the extra effort I was putting in was making a difference in the life of someone that had already given up on living.

Still that burning question was always in the back of my head. "Why was I so happy? Was I born with a positive "glass is half full" attitude? Was it forced? Was it a learned behavior?" I wasn't sure but I had to find out. So, with that I slowly started to research the topic and do some very deep soul searching.

My first search was simply the definition of happiness............. Happiness is a state of mind or feeling characterized by contentment, love, satisfaction, pleasure or joy. I think it's safe to say that everyone in this world wants to be happy. As human beings the search for happiness can be a lifelong journey. In a world filled with poverty, war, disease, death and injustice on every level, it's no wonder anyone is happy at all. It can appear difficult to see the positive things we have going for us, instead, focusing on the negative.

In my research I learned that the world has been searching for the meaning of happiness since the beginning of time. One of the most interesting observations of happiness came from Greek philosopher Aristotle (394-322 B.C). (For more information, visit www.catholic education. org)

Aristotle came to the conclusion that no person deliberately chooses to be happy. So, if this is the case then human beings wish to be happy, and the search for happiness leads us to look at what kinds of happiness there might be and whether these types are logical.

Aristotle's theory was that there are four types of happiness:

1. Latus: Happiness is a thing. "I'm addicted to peanut butter ice cream, I see it, I eat it, I feel good, I'm happy." This principal is based on something external from ones self, it is short lived and is more for immediate satisfaction.

2. Felix: Happiness is comparative advantage. "I have more than X; therefore I am better than X". This kind of happiness results from competition with another person. The

self is seen in terms of how we measure up to others. This form of happiness is rather unstable and if one fails, can lead to a sense of worthlessness.

3. Beatitudo: This form of happiness comes from seeing the good in others and doing good for others. Most people would prefer a world structured around the pursuit of happiness # 3, than entirely based on happiness # 2. This idea proves that people are more good than bad. The problem with this form of happiness is that it is limited. We cannot be someone else's everything. For example, they or we will eventually die and if our happiness is contingent on them, then it dies with them.

4. Sublime Beautudo: This level is the most difficult to describe. It encompasses a reach for fullness and perfection of happiness. This is the category in which some leave it up to a higher power with the recognition that certain things are beyond what we are capable of doing purely on our own.

This all sounds good in theory, but why was I so happy and Leo so miserable? I was beginning to think that circumstance had a lot to do with how we act, relate to others, and deal with our own misfortunes.

During numerous conversations with Leo, I had come to find out that he had made some poor choices in his personal life that lead to his dismal attitude and lack of drive to survive. Each day I tried to shed light into his dreary world until one day he began to smile again. And though his medical condition worsened each day, his attitude seemed to be getting better. He began telling me stories from his childhood, and trips he had taken. One day, while listening outside his door, I even heard him tell his physician about trips he had taken to Aruba and the beautiful women he had met. And for a brief moment I heard him laugh. To this day, I have never felt such a sense of accomplishment in my professional life.

From that moment on, I became increasingly aware of the profound impact health care professionals have on their patients. I spent countless hours observing my coworkers and their relationships with the patients they cared for. I witnessed random acts of human kindness that would bring even the toughest soul to tears. And I began to realize that in years of working in numerous other fields, I had just been going through the motions without ever feeling the affect of touching the lives of others. And while the medical field is not for everyone, this was where I belonged.

Stop, listen, and take the time

Anyone that has ever worked in the health care field can tell you just how stressful it can be. With high acuity levels and heavy patient loads, often times medical personnel feel as if the care they are giving is inadequate, but may be unsure of how to change the environment in which they are working in. Thus, stress levels are heightened.

The patients we deal with are often times scared, confused and frustrated. I have heard countless patients express the fact that they feel as if they are being pushed aside and not given enough information about their illness. On the flip side, I have observed numerous nurses complaining about the fact that there is just not enough time in a day to give the proper care that they know their patients deserve.

We all get so caught up with the technical element of patient care and our own personal routines that we often times forget about the human aspect of our job. Healthcare is far more than a diagnosis and medical treatment. If we truly want to perform our jobs to the best of our ability we need to STOP, LISTEN, and TAKE THE TIME to get to know our patients. For they are the very reason we have a job in the first place. But it goes much deeper than that.

During my three short years in the medical field I have met numerous types of people. Every race, creed, nationality, religion...you name it, I have seen it all. And just when I think I have seen everything, something else surprises me. But one thing always remains the same. People are most receptive when you genuinely take the time to get to know them. There are some that would argue that there is a fine line and that you shouldn't ever share personal information with your patients but I couldn't disagree more. I believe that if you exercise common sense and discretion you will be far more successful at building a rapport with your patients.

Often times it means checking your agenda at the door and following the lead of your patient. This technique may be difficult for many, including myself but it is a crucial element that is often necessary in order for us to perform our jobs successfully.

Early one morning I rushed into a patient's room, greeted him with a smile, and started rambling on about what the plan was for the day. It was 7 A.M and my morning had been extremely stressful already and I knew I had a lot to accomplish in a short amount of time. I began to inadvertently rush the patient. Explaining to him that it would be a good idea if he got out of bed for breakfast and told him that I could get him the supplies that he needed if he wanted to shower before he ate.

He took one long look at me, said nothing and just smiled. At first I thought that he didn't hear me so I asked him again, only in a louder voice. Again, no response. I began to suggest other options to get him motivated to start his day and he stopped me dead in my tracks. He looked me straight in the eye and said, "It's clear you have an agenda for the day and I wouldn't want to throw you off. I will do whatever you ask of me." I just stood there in silence. What was I thinking? These people are sick and all I am doing is barking orders. I felt ashamed.

I then sat in the chair next to his bed, grabbed his hand and apologized for my erratic behavior. We sat there and talked for a few minutes and I began to ask him questions about his background, and family. I must have been talking a mile a minute. Probably due to the fact that I was completely embarrassed of how I had approached him that morning.

While I sat there rambling on, he reached out and put his hand on my shoulder. Then he said, "Honey, the world won't stop if your ship is set off its course". At first I was offended and tried to think of a snappy come back, but I knew that he was right. I tried to apologize again for making him feel rushed but he wouldn't have it. He merely suggested that I should move slower and be aware that not everyone in the hospital will always fit into my schedule and that I should really take the time to get to know each patient.

He also stated that when I dashed into his room with a "gang-banger attitude" he felt ambushed and before he knew it, he was putty in my hands. It was clear to him that my day was planned out long before I even walked into his room and he didn't want to upset me by throwing me off track.

Later that day he mentioned that he had been a psychiatrist for 50 years and it was his job to study human behavior. He said that he was able to size me up within 5 minutes of meeting me and while he knew I was a good person, I needed to be reminded of the fact that it wasn't all about me.

I felt horrible. But I knew he was speaking the truth. Up until that point I felt that I had been doing a fantastic job caring for my patients. However, I was beginning to understand the fact that in order to be successful at my job, I had to give up one thing. Control. Control of the illusion that every piece of my day had to be planned out. My schedule for each day was not carved in stone.

In this line of work we are dealing with people that are ill and that have lost control over their health, body, and even sometimes their mind. Some have been given a terminal diagnosis. Others have lost the use of certain bodily functions. And there are those that have even lost their will to live.

As health care professionals, we have a direct impact on those we care for. We hold the power to give them choices while they are staying with us. We need to stop and take the time to genuinely get to know our patients.

In the hustle and bustle of our day, it is necessary that we keep in mind that these are human beings that we are dealing with. And the next time you find yourself becoming frustrated because of the fact that things are not going according to your "master plan". Stop and ask yourself, "Is it really going to matter at the end of the day what order I do things in?" As humans it is impossible to control the actions of others, but is absolutely essential to control our need to plan out every aspect of our day while at work. We need to spend ample time learning about our patients and more importantly, LISTENING to them.

Wisdom

Lets face it; over 75% of the general hospital population is elderly. This group of patients is particularly unique and deserve to be treated with the highest degree of respect. However, it has been my experience that this is the population of patients that is most often neglected.

I once overheard a nurse telling her coworker, "He's 92 years old; there isn't much I can do for him. He's just lucky he has made it this long". Now that may be true, but it surely doesn't mean that just because this gentleman can't be rehabilitated, we should just write him off, let him sit in his room alone, and forget about him.

In my opinion, our elderly population deserve more time and attention than our other patients. Think about it. What type of care would you expect for your grandparents or even parents? These patients are often confused, frightened, and depressed. Why shouldn't we take extra time to get to know them and explain in detail what is happening to them?

Often it comes down to time, or lack there of. Most of the elderly are hard of hearing and often times their minds aren't as sharp as they once were. They may have a memory deficiency, or have trouble communicating with us. All of this can be frustrating but we must learn to take the time. At the very least, we owe it to them. Even if you have to explain the same thing fifty times, please treat these people with respect. They are human beings and deserve our compassion and understanding.

These patients are often times desperate for any kind of human contact. A lot of them have come from nursing homes or from living alone in their own homes. Some have recently lost a spouse and with that, their will to live. Try to relate to these people. You would be amazed at the stories they can tell, and wisdom they are just dying to share with someone that will genuinely take the time to listen. Most countries embrace their elders. Why, in this country are they forgotten?

Just last week I had a patient in her mid-seventies with advanced dementia. When I arrived at work that morning I heard screaming and crying, only to find out that it was her. I dropped what I was doing, went straight to her room, identified myself, and then grabbed her hand. It took at least five minutes to bring her down to a level where I could clearly comprehend what she was saying. She was extremely upset that her watch was missing and was convinced that our staff had stolen it.

I told her that I would ask the night shift if they had seen it and call the emergency room to see if she had left it there. When I asked my coworkers, a few of them laughed and hinted that because of her confused state, she had no idea what she was talking about. Maybe so, but I couldn't shake the feeling that there was truth to what she was saying. She seemed so adamant about having the watch when she arrived at the hospital; I knew I had to keep looking.

We must have looked for that watch for hours. Just when I was about to give up, I found it in a bag under a blanket in her room. The look on her face was priceless. After thanking me, she shared the tearful story of how that same watch had been given to her by her father when she was fifteen, just before he passed away.

I was completely blown away. Just because someone has dementia doesn't mean they can't have moments of lucidity. I walked with my head up a little higher that day. It was something so simple to me, but I knew that I had made a difference in the life of someone that was merely trying to hold onto something familiar.

Every one of our patients has something to contribute, but the elderly have seen things that you or I have only read about. So, strike up a conversation. Create a bond with your patient. You may be surprised with how something so small can make such a difference in the care we provide for our patients and the degree of compliance they reciprocate.

Through the eyes of a child

No one can show us the power of happiness like a child. Children just seem to wake up in a good mood. They seldom exhibit signs of stress and have the most beautiful smiles. They love unconditionally and have an uncanny way of brightening even the darkest days.

Earlier this year I had the brief opportunity of working at a large children's hospital. During my stint I was caring for extremely ill children, most of which had life threatening conditions. These kids were much sicker than the adults that I had taken care of, but you would never know.

It is quite possible that these children couldn't comprehend just how sick they really were, but I'd like to think that it's more than that. You see, children see the world in a very matter of fact way. They live in the moment and appreciate things for what they are. They speak their minds and are very receptive to the feelings of others. Especially their parents.

I believe that if a child senses hurt or pain displayed by an adult in their life, they instinctively act as if nothing is wrong. They carry on through the pain. They continue to laugh, love, and play. Often times pretending that everything is just as it should be. In my opinion, children are not given enough credit for their instinct and intuitiveness. They are naturally happy and embrace the world around them. If only that innocence didn't vanish the older we get.

When working in this delicate field of health care, it is important to remember not to feel sorry for these children. You can empathize and exercise extra compassion, but do it in a positive manner. Children need to feel protected. They have every right to be informed of their illness and to have the details condensed to an age appropriate level so they can comprehend all that is happening to them. We owe it to them to stay upbeat and positive.

I will never forget a two-year-old little girl named Madison. She had a rare form of cancer that was rapidly taking over her little body. From the moment I met her, I knew she would forever touch my soul.

Madison was the happiest child I had ever met with a smile that lit up the room. The only thing that separated her from the other kids was that Madison didn't have a family that stayed with her or even came to visit. You see, Madison was an orphan. She had bounced between foster families for the first eighteen months of her life and when Madison became ill, no one seemed to want her.

You would never know by looking at her, what a tough start to life this beautiful little girl had. Each day I worked,

Madison and I became closer. I would spend my lunch break holding her and playing with her. And on the days that she was too sick to hold her head up, I would rock her to sleep. I couldn't help but think that this was probably the most genuine contact she had ever had with another human being. And it saddened me.

Just when I started to feel bad for her, Madison would sense it and do something to make me laugh. She was a regular comedian and the other kids adored her. Given her desperate situation, she never once felt sorry for herself.

Two months later, Madison lost her battle. It wasn't until she was gone, did I realize just how many lives that little angel had touched. Including mine. And though Madison was only on this planet for two short years, she taught me a valuable life-long lesson. I learned that no matter how grim the situation appears, to never give up hope or your zest for life. We, as health care workers possess the power to make others smile. And if we see the world through the eyes of a child, we will learn to appreciate the small things in life and make the very best of even the most difficult situation. If Madison could do it, so can we.

The power of touch

It is impossible in the field of health care to make it through your day without having to touch someone. Now, I'm not talking about touching their lives indirectly. I'm speaking of physically reaching out and touching your patients.

It amazes me when I come across someone in this line of work that cringes at the thought of physical contact. I mean, this is what our job entails. Physical touch is more than skin-deep. Skin is the human body's largest organ, containing millions of receptors. There are roughly 8000 in a single fingertip. They send messages through nerve fibers connected to the spinal cord and then to the brain. A simple touch on the hand or shoulder can reduce the heart rate and blood pressure. Even deep coma patients may show changes in their pulse when their hands are held. Positive nurturing touch appears to stimulate the release of endorphins, the body's natural pain suppressors. That may explain why a father's hug can literally "make it better" when a child skins his knee. Or a suffering premature baby can't thrive without touch.

Research shows that touch sends a message that boosts immune function and create lower levels of the stress hormones cortisol and norepinephrine. Since every one of our patients are stressed just by being in the hospital, shouldn't we want to do everything in our power to minimize their anxiety? A stress-free patient is a manageable patient.

Some patients who are undergoing treatments for cancer and other devastating illnesses are opting to give the benefits of human touch a try. Also known as touch therapy. Slight movements of the fingers and palms of massage therapists help to renew the spirit and restore harmony in the bodies of those who are suffering. An increased immune system, quicker recovery times following chemotherapy, relief from depression, and increased circulation are among the many benefits that have been reported by those who choose to reap the benefits of human touch.

Often times our patients are feeling helpless and hopeless. And though we may have no control over their illness, we do have the power to offer comfort. Whether it is holding a hand, rubbing a back, brushing tangled hair, helping with a sponge bath or giving a kind hug, we owe it to our patients to offer any type of support and affection we can.

The beautiful thing about the power of touch is that this type of comfort doesn't require words to be effective.

I think back to a thirty-five year old patient of mine that had just undergone a complete hysterectomy. When she arrived from surgery, numerous friends and family all there to offer support surrounded her. This woman appeared so strong and unaffected by what had just transpired. She laughed and joked with her family and appeared as if she hadn't a care in the world.

After a few hours, her visitors decided to leave so that she could get some rest. I went into her room a few moments later, only to find her crouched in the fetal position, and sobbing uncontrollably. I stood by her bed frozen. Unable to speak, I thought to myself, "Was this the same women that had seemed so strong a few minutes ago?" Finally, instinct took over and I sat on the edge of her bed, held her hand, and began rubbing her back. I sat there for at least fifteen minutes comforting her, as if I would a close friend. But not a word was spoken. In spite of the twenty other things on my agenda, I knew that I needed to sit with her for as long as it took. This was a woman not much older than me, with no children, and now no way of conceiving her own. I began to imagine what must have been going through her head and I began to cry with her. I felt her broken spirit, her feelings of inadequacy, her lost dreams, and elements of womanhood that had been stripped from her.

I then realized that there was nothing I could say to make her pain go away, so I bent down, gave her a comforting hug, and held her for what seemed like an eternity. I knew that was just what she needed and I was right.

She then, began to pull herself together and asked me a question I wasn't prepared to answer. She wiped her tears and said, "How did you know?" I told her that sometimes there is nothing more that can be said. Nothing I could have said to her would have eased her pain, so I just let my body take over and comfort her in the only way I knew how. She then thanked me for giving her the opportunity to "break-down" and told me that she appreciated the fact that I didn't discourage her, yet I offered unconditional support. I assured her that the behavior that she had displayed was both healthy and normal for the ordeal she had been through and it was okay to "break down".

From that moment on, I have learned how to do less talking and more listening. I now realize that the phrase "actions speak louder than words" has true meaning. Everyday I'm increasingly aware that sometimes the best option is to just say nothing but be there physically. There is nothing on this earth more meaningful than the power of human touch and nothing as healing.

Change your thought process

We are all creatures of habit and routine. The way we think, relate to others, and carry ourselves is usually not well thought out. It is human nature to put the people we meet into categories within seconds of coming into contact with them. Hopefully what I'm about to share with you, will help you relate to every one of your patients differently.

I arrived at work early one morning and received a run down from the night shift on my patients for the day. I was informed of a certain patient that I was told would be a "problem" because all she wanted was pain medication and I was told that when she didn't get it on time, she became irate and hostile. Now, anyone in the field of medicine knows this type of patient well. We put them in the category "narc seeker". Someone that, for whatever reason is addicted to pain medication and often times comes to the hospital once their prescription runs out.

I thought to myself, "Great, can't I go at least one day without one of these drug seeking cases?" I decided to enter to her room first, introduce myself, and find out what I could do for her. When I got there, I could barely get my name out before she began asking me for more pain medication. I told her the same thing that I tell every one of my pain med seeking patients. "I'm not sure if it's time for anymore medicine, but I will ask your nurse." Now I will admit that there may have been a slight brash tone to my voice, but I had seen this "type" of patient a million times before, and I didn't have much sympathy for them. I couldn't have been more wrong.

The woman began to sob and asked me to come to her bedside. I then sat in a chair next to her bed as she held her hand out to shake mine. She then told me her name and asked me a few questions about myself. Then she looked me dead in the eye and said, "Kristin, do you have any idea what it is like to live with chronic pain every second of every day of your life?" I told her that I didn't know what it was like because I had always been extremely healthy. Then she began to tell me about her debilitating disease called Lupus. She stated that she would give anything to even go an hour without any form of medication or pain. I couldn't have felt worse. Here was a woman that legitimately needed help controlling her pain, and I just threw here into a category and treated her like a drug addict.

She went on to tell me just how active she had been all of her life until one day she started aching and the pain never went away. She then shared with me the fact that every day she would rather take her own life than to consume the small pharmacy of medications that help her function on a minimal level. She informed me that she had three young children that she was raising alone due to the fact that her husband of fifteen years lost his battle with cancer just four months earlier. At this point I felt about three inches tall. "How dare I put her into a category without knowing her full story? Who was I to decide whether this woman was truly in pain or needed medication? How could I be so cold?"

The woman noticed that I was tearing up and reached over and grabbed my hand. She then told me that she didn't mean to upset me and that she saw something special within me and felt like she needed to share her story. She was right, while I consider myself full of compassion and empathy for my patients; I had unknowingly become a victim of my environment. Meaning, I had started putting my patients into little sub categories based on my past experiences. This doesn't mean that there won't always be that population of drug seeking patients that abuse various medications. But what it now means for me is that I truly needed to change my thought process. It means that we, as health care professionals should make a conscious effort not to stereotype our patients. They are all human beings, and as much as we would like to think we know someone's background, we have no clue. It's all about interpretation, and things are not always as they seem.

Change your thought process and you will change your world.

Physicians who truly care

In my short time in the medical field, I have mastered the skill of making the distinction between the physicians who truly care for their patients, the ones who went to medical school for all the wrong reasons, and those that are simply "burnt out".

Just like the rest of us in this field, physicians too have high patient loads and limited time to perform the duties that are expected of them. I have heard it said many times that since physicians receive high salaries they don't deserve all that much sympathy. I strongly disagree.

What people fail to realize is that physicians deserve every penny they earn. We are quick to forget just how much work and personal sacrifice physicians must endure to obtain those initials behind their name. The countless hours of studying, testing, and working as residents with very little pay. The monstrous student loans that most of them are still paying off. Not to mention the expensive yet necessary malpractice insurance. Sure, this career will be extremely profitable for them in the long run, but it can take years to pay off their debt from the education they received.

I have had the pleasure of working with some of the most generous, compassionate, and knowledgeable physicians in the field. I have witnessed physicians going out of their way to help patients on a daily basis. Most of them truly practice empathy and offer comfort to even their sickest patients.

I just think that there are many misconceptions out there that should really be addressed. I'm not saying that all physicians treat others with respect and dignity, but that is not only relative to those in the medical field. Where would we be without experienced physicians? It is clearly not a job for everyone, but then again, how many of us would have the drive, perseverance, or discipline to devote to an education for eleven or more years?

My uncle Danny is a perfect example of how compassionate physicians have the power to enhance the quality of life for their patients.

My uncle had smoked since as far back as I can remember and at age forty-nine, it sadly caught up with him. After feeling ill for several months, he decided to go to the doctor. He assumed that he probably had pneumonia or a horrible virus that he just couldn't kick. He surely wasn't prepared to hear what was truly taking over his body.

Danny's physician delivered the news that no one wants to hear. "Mr. Hall, you have stage four lung cancer and the prognosis isn't good. We can fight it but realistically we give you three to six months". In all of my life, I could never imagine what hearing those words would feel like.

But Danny wouldn't go down without a fight. Within days he began intense radiation and chemotherapy. Danny's physicians never discouraged him, yet stood beside him every step of the way. They were well aware of the statistics, but continued to offer numerous options and hope. You see, Danny had goals. First of which, was seeing his only child graduate and then a bittersweet farewell to boot camp. My uncle Dan was there for those momentous occasions, and made precious memories with his son and family. He just wasn't ready to go yet, and continued to fight.

Days turned into months and Danny's condition worsened. Each test revealed the grim news that the cancer was spreading. He moved forward with his treatments as the doctors tried to keep him as comfortable and as pain free as possible.

When his family offered to take him in for the remainder of his life, Danny refused. Partially because he didn't want to be a burden, but mostly because he would be too far from the doctors that he adored. He had such a talented and compassionate group of physicians, he just couldn't bear the thought of starting over with a new set of doctors. He was well aware of his bleak reality and worried that if he went elsewhere he would hear that dreaded phrase, "Sorry, but there is nothing else we can do for you".

This is just one of the many examples I have witnessed regarding the bond between physicians and their patients. I have seen them offer money to the poor, deliver laughter during times of need, and shed tears when feeling helpless when there was nothing more that could be done.

We must remember that physicians are only human. They make mistakes. They have bad days. They sometimes feel overwhelmed like you and I. But they deserve the same understanding, compassion, and respect you would give any other coworker. After all, we are all in this together, and it is so very important that we work as a team in the best interest of our patients.

Ali's Story

Every once in a while someone comes along and changes your life forever. My good friend Allison was that someone for me.

It was 2:30 A.M when I received a call that still haunts me to this day. It was my friend Ali and she was sobbing uncontrollably. "The test results came back positive Krist, I have stage four cervical cancer and it is spreading...they gave me six months to a year to live". Was this just a bad dream or a morbid reality? "I'll be right there", I said. With that, I threw a few things in a bag and jumped in the car heading towards Ali's house near Chicago. It was just an hour drive but it seemed like an eternity. On the drive down, I began to reminisce. My mind raced back ten years when Ali and I first met, and how we always joked that it felt like we had known each other all of our lives. I then remembered how many crazy times we had shared and how no one had ever made me laugh as hard as her. I thought back to the night I introduced her to her now ex-husband, their wedding and the birth of their beautiful daughter Antonia. How could this be happening? Her life was being cut too short.

I arrived around 4 A.M, walked into the house, went up the stairs to Ali's bedroom, and just stood there. Neither of us could say a word. I walked over to her bed, sat down, and threw my arms around her. "Honey, you'll get through this", I said. And both of us cried for hours.

And for the next fourteen months, that is exactly what she did, she got through it. It wasn't pretty, it wasn't pleasant, but she got through it. I spent most of my days off with Ali and her daughter, and always tried to focus on the positive. When she lost weight, we would joke about the fact that she never had to take another spinning class. When her hair fell out in clumps, we went wig shopping and turned her into a beautiful blonde. And when she was too weak to move, we would both lie on the couch all day and eat ice cream.

Ali continued to fight each day for that little glimmer of hope that someday this would all go away. Two months before she passed away, I surprised her with a trip to Vegas. It was just like old times. Laughing, joking and pretending that this wasn't good-bye. But we both knew better.

The day Ali left this earth was one of the hardest days of my life. Her ex-husband, mother, and I spent the entire day at her hospital bedside. We reminisced and assured Ali that we would all see that her daughter was well taken care of. We told her that it is alright to go and that she didn't have to suffer anymore.

Then Ali requested that everyone but me leave the room. She then reached for my hand and squeezed it with every last ounce of strength she had. She began telling me that she wanted to thank me for being the positive up-beat person that I am. She went on to tell me that it really made a difference in her attitude and will to live. Ali said that she wanted me to deliver her eulogy at her funeral and only talk about the positive aspects of her life. She stated that I was the only person that never for even one second treated her like she was sick, and because of that she felt the need to keep fighting. Ali said, "Everyone has a gift and yours is the ability to turn any negative into a positive and then spread that joy to others. Don't ever change for anyone." Those were the last words she ever spoke to me.

A few minutes later my beautiful friend Allison took her last breath. I was filled with mixed emotions. I was grateful that she wasn't suffering anymore, yet devastated because I had just lost one of my best friends. I was fearful that Antonia would never know just how wonderful, compassionate, and brilliant her mother really was. That she would never know just how much she lit up the room with her mere presence. And that she had been robbed of having that unconditional comfort that only a mother can offer.

It has been nearly a year since Ali's death and I still think of her often. Each day I strive to continue being that up-beat positive person that Ali knew and loved. I always felt like I was a happy person but Ali helped me realize that these qualities are appreciated by others as well. Life isn't always perfect, but it's all about how you handle your misfortunes and how quickly you bounce back.

Take time for YOU

No matter what job you have it is always good practice to take time out for you. However, as a medical professional it should be a requirement to take time to rejuvenate. There are not many other careers in which the decisions you make have such an impact on the lives of others and may literally mean the difference between life and death.

Often times medical personnel work extremely long shifts and many hours per week. It is necessary that we spend enough time away from our working environment in order to be successful at our jobs. It is next to impossible to take care of someone else without taking care of yourself first.

For myself, for two straight years, I worked anywhere from seventy-ninety hours per week. Often times pulling several sixteen-hour shifts in a row with only five hours of sleep each night. My friends, family, and coworkers all thought I was insane, but the truth was, that I had just gotten used to it. At the time I didn't see the effects it was having on my personal life and even the quality of care that I was giving to my patients. I have since reduced my hours and can't even begin to tell you what a profound change it has made in my life.

The first thing I can suggest is to laugh. I mean truly laugh out loud and often. Laugh with your coworkers as well as your patients. The phrase "laughter is the best medicine" has become a cliché because it is so true. We know that laughter has benefits far beyond mood. Laughter can actually enhance immunity and prolong life. Maintaining a sense of humor about the trials and tribulations of life can bring continual happiness, as well as less stress.

So, what do I mean when I say take time for you? It can be something as simple as taking a walk outside at lunch or getting away for a fifteen-minute break to check your email. It might mean making cookies with your kids or taking a bubble bath with your significant other. For those of you whom are desperate for "alone" time, I would suggest getting a relaxing massage twice per month or going on a long run. For us women, you may even need to go on a shopping spree with your girlfriends or have a "chick flick" night. For men, maybe take up a new hobby or sport. Whatever you decide is just fine, as long as it gets your mind away from work.

It's amazing what a little time off can do. When you arrive back at work, you feel rejuvenated and more relaxed. You can look at each day with promise and hope. Trust me, your patients will notice and thank you for it. You know it's not a good thing when your patients start asking you if you live at the hospital, because they never see you leave.

Here are a few of my favorite stress relievers

- Eating ice cream while taking a long hot bath

- "People watching" at a nearby park or busy airport

- Finger painting with a child

- Dancing naked in your living room

- Wrestling with your dog

- Screaming at the top of your lungs at a live sporting event

- Sex (by far, the best stress reliever I know)

- Climbing a mountain

- Writing in a journal

- Pedicures

- Yoga

- Cooking

- A long drive without a particular destination

- Going to the salon for a new haircut or color

- Any form of SHOPPING (you can't get much more therapeutic than that)

- LAUGHING

- Three-day weekends

- Swimming

- Calling an old friend out of the blue and talking for hours

- Filling your mouth with 5 pieces of bubble gum and then blowing the biggest bubble you can

- Volunteering time to those who could really use the help

- Spending time with a grandparent

- Meditation

- Joining a class that you would have never joined in a million years, just because you are curious

- Gardening

- Washing your car (by hand)

- Going to a movie alone

- Singing loudly in your car with the windows down

- Treating a homeless person to lunch and taking the time to get to know them

- Donating to your favorite local charity

- Buying lemonade from a child's lemonade stand

- Sitting somewhere peaceful and thinking about how lucky you are

The end yet just the beginning

Now back to the reason I decided to write this book. Remember my patient Leo, from the beginning of the story? Leo lost his battle nearly two months after he was hospitalized. I remember how hard I took the loss, but told few about the affect it had on me as a person and how I struggled with the fact that I had gotten so close to one of my patients.

For me, that was the hardest part. Not the fact that Leo was gone, but the fact that I had allowed myself to get so attached. I was beginning to wonder if I should keep a safe distance from my future patients and just remain professional. This way, I was still fulfilling my duties as a health care provider, while delivering superb care, but without affecting my emotions. I decided to give it a try and it lasted almost a month. Until the day I received a letter that changed my mind once again.

Upon arriving at work early one morning the unit clerk handed me a letter and on the front it said, "To: Little

Miss Sunshine". This was the nickname that Leo had given me. My heart sank and tears filled my eyes. I knew exactly where this letter had come from and I was scared to open it. I waited twelve hours until I was finished with work and then decided to read it in my car.

It was written by Leo's caregiver and friend. She was one of the only people that had come to visit Leo while he was hospitalized and it was obvious just how much she cared for him. In the letter she started out by simply thanking me for the extra time that I had spent with Leo. She wanted me to realize just how much of an impact I had on his day-to-day life while he was in the hospital.

She went on to give specific examples about how I obtained special permission from Leo's doctor to take him down to the hospital cafeteria and let him deviate from his strict renal diet. She also praised me for putting him in a wheelchair and taking him on walks every chance I could. She just wanted me to know that the extra "little" things that I did for Leo had not gone unnoticed.

Unbeknown to me, she and Leo had several in depth conversations about the fact that I was the happiest person that he had ever met. And as much as he hated to admit it, he knew that I truly cared for him and it was my positive attitude that helped him get through numerous days while he lay in bed depressed and wanting nothing more than to die.

This letter touched me deeply and I felt a profound sense of accomplishment. Here I was, just one person out of entire team of health care professionals that had been a part of Leo's care, yet I never gave up on him. It reminded me of a quote that I had once heard, "To the world you may be just one person. But to one person you may be the world". That quote is a true testimony of what I had been to Leo.

I then came to the realization that our patients need us to been there on a personal level. This doesn't mean having to create such a bond with every patient that we become incapable of separating ourselves emotionally. It simply means using our intuition to find those special patients that need a little extra compassion. We should also keep in mind that compassion doesn't necessarily have to come in the form of words. A smile with your eyes, holding a hand, or a gentle hug are all acts of kindness that say, "I care, I'm here for you, and I value you as a person".

This book is simply titled Happiness in Healthcare because having a positive attitude is absolutely pivotal in this field. No matter what hardships you are facing in your personal life, or how badly your day is going, please remember that our patients have it worse. It takes a strong individual to put on a happy face when things may not be going according to plan. But it takes an even stronger person to step outside of your world and recognize that life is much more than personal happiness. We all possess the profound power of positive energy to share with each and every soul we encounter, while working in the rewarding field of health care, and living this beautiful life that we have been given.

Thank you for taking the time to read my story.

Acknowledgments

First off, I would like to thank my mother. I was a very energetic, strong willed, and defiant child. She always told me that if I used all that energy for good, I would be very successful at whatever I set my mind to. How's this Mom? I also owe a huge thank you to my stepfather Gary for always adding an element of humor each and every day, since he entered my life at the age of nine. I really need to thank my baby brother Eric, for putting up with my eccentric ways. Eric, your overprotective sister loves you very much and I never want you to forget just how much I believe in you. You are brilliant and one of the most thoughtful people I know. NEVER underestimate yourself or give up on your dreams! Also, a thank you to my loving grandparents. Grandma B., you and I are kindred spirits and I have always adored you for your positive energy and crazy antics. My Papa, you are the kindest soul I know. You will always be my "Mr. Fix-It", and I love you very much! You both have always believed in me and supported me through thick and thin. THANK YOU!!

Grandma C, one of my earliest memories of you is that infectious laugh. You have endured many trying times and always seem to come out on top. Though we are miles apart, please know that I think of you often and I am a better person for the life lessons that you have taught me. And, many thanks to numerous other family members for your support, and providing many laughs throughout the years. We have had some good times, haven't we? Thank you to each and every one of my friends. My life is just a little better because each of you are a part of it. A special thank you to Jennie, Joe, Tia, and Ashton. Thank you for making me just a little less O.C.D and also for helping me through the darkest point of my life. You are like my second family and I would do anything for you! Tell Tia and Ashton that I am an ADULT, not a KID! I love you! A gigantic thank you to my Mercy Maniacs. Without having the pleasure of working with you, this book would not have the same meaning. You all made my experience at Mercy extremely worthwhile. Tina and Lisa (my Mercy Den Mothers), thank you both for never taking me too seriously, and for accepting and loving me for who I truly am. Joell, all I can say is that we have had some interesting times while working together…thank you for your contagious laughter. Tawana, thank you for being that strong woman we all know and love. Did your "special" swing arrive yet? Crissy, you are my sweetheart, and I am very proud of my new little RN! Kitty, your biscuit is right here.. Come and get some. Julie, I love your sarcastic nature. You can be my paramedic anytime. Kathy, take good care of my boyfriend Vinnie. Kristy, hubba-hubba. Penny W., my uncle Chuck is still single if you are interested. Christine K., I love your confidence.

Penny I., how many copies would you like to buy for your new employees? Paula, where does that arrow to lead again? Michelle S., you have been on both ends of the spectrum, and practice true empathy while caring for your patients. I admire your humor, and courage. Barb, this is our World Series year!! Peggy, I will never forget your support throughout the Larry ordeal. Thank you. Kristin and Tricia, GO CUBBIES!! Linda, I wish you knew just how much your patients appreciate all that you do for them. You are a saint. Kim, take care of those boys. Amy, ready for some karaoke? Michelle B., love that smile! Dr. Szekely, thank you for always taking the time to listen and offer advice. Let me know if your band ever makes it big. I would tell everyone, "I knew him when…". Dr. Shamsee, you are a wonderful physician and add a "clam" element to the hospitalist world. Dr. Shihadeh, your talent extends far beyond what is noticed by others. Stay positive and never cut that hair (kidding, of course). Dr. Al Hamwi, congrats on #7. Dr. M. Kahn, it's obvious that you enjoy your job. Congrats on that beautiful baby. Dr. Konkol, you are my hero. Anyone that diagnoses and treats that many infectious diseases deserves a metal. Keep up the good work. Dr. Sharma, the bond that you have with your patients is undeniable. Also, thank you to my coworkers at Littleton Adventist Hospital, and St. Francis Hospital. It has been my pleasure working with each and every one of you.

LaVergne, TN USA
21 June 2010
186831LV00001B/11/P